THE WONDER YEARS

For more information:
Stephen F. Austin State University Press
P.O. Box 13007 SFA Station
Nacogdoches, Texas 75962
sfapress@sfasu.edu
www.sfasu.edu/sfapress

Managing Editor: Kimberly Verhines
Book design: Arian Katsimbras
Cover design: Hannah DeHaven & Arian Katsimbras
Cover image: Arian Katsimbras

Distributed by Texas A&M Consortium
www.tamupress.com

ISBN: 978-1-62288-239-7

THE WONDER YEARS

Arian Katsimbras

STEPHEN F. AUSTIN STATE UNIVERSITY PRESS

For the boy and his universe heart.

CONTENTS

My Mother and Father Were Astronauts

THE WONDER YEARS

My Mother and Father Were Astronauts

My mother in the background
        with a trade wind held in her face.
Her carmine hair
      laid blade straight on a table's edge. Gravity there, too,
                  with its promise
      to pull her headfirst
       through the photo's bottom, where the edges ghost
her skin to near transparence; the brink of the world
              threatens to erase her
more darkly. Her mother is a distance
       birthing loudly. Her mother is a body inside
          out; a basement of Old Milwaukee cans.
My grandfather levitates
behind us. He holds a leaking carburetor.   No, it's bloodfruit
     pulled from a hole in his chest – grease-pitted Amarillo hands
        holding it like a newborn
    offering to some ancient god. As he died, he sang
   say the black, say the black, say the black. It's the little things
that make us ordinary
        as coal, starved as the back
   of a dog's mouth. I no longer know the other man pictured
   holding me
toward the sky in a gesture of Saturn
            eating his sons.
Four gold rings
    on his fingers – a constellation on my half-formed body
       – which he will later call down
from an indifferent sky
     repeatedly and beat into me before leaving
        all of us for good,

for god,

for dust and dust, for South Dakota's Badlands,

and I'll be left with a rag

to clean the shit off my little brother's

tender too thin skin;

his bad mouth giving up

teeth the way space opens and meteors   confuse the sky,

but without the splendor, flourish, dying javelins

of light. Little brother

with shattered teeth. Little orbiting boy radiating at my knees

until I too lift him up

like a father and son, kiss soft his howling mouth,

until in time each tooth falls out,

until our mother comes back

from an emptiness   she's spent so much time

being loved and undone by and takes us both

down from out the sky,

out his fists. Barroom myths of my stepfather

make him god-sized, boulders

for hands, a tower of light

emanating from atop a spinepile,

a world eater. After he left, what took in his absence

was a fuss   of leashed dogs

branched out from a fencepost in the backyard, each one

a cruel blossom for a mouth in want

for bone knots

We ornamented the bathroom stalls

with each graffitied version of his death: he became

a mobile home, singlewide, every window

shot through

with neighborhood rocks; he became

a handful of stone; he became

a windstorm that pulled the house
                        from its cinders and scabbed earth,
used his body like sackcloth to rub the sky clean
                of the crushed stars for a night; he became
                        the currency of the desert,
its careful blood
calculus. Time took back everything it gave me.
            The mule in the adjacent lot eloped with brushfire, and I,
too, imagined becoming
                        an unforgiving eater,
            find my father dried out
in the labyrinthine rabbitbrush
                                and eat and eat
or find him chained to a poplar for birds to come
                and split their beaks on
            and he'd split his mouth, too, to mirror them and glisten
                (o' radiance, o' carrion, o' namesake),
        whose slick mouths hold scissors,
                        and we'd forget which one
to call by its proper name. Him? They? What is a murder
            if not a chorus of mouths singing
the same hunger? And so, I became hunger.
                    I came to know the halo
        of my blushing boy head as nothing
                    more than the dim lightbulb
he raised me toward in the last picture.
                        These were the wonder years.
An atlas born of the sound glass
            makes when hexed to life
                by a boy with a rock.
            The truth is.
            The truth is

a man in South Dakota with blood in his pockets,
     blood in the fringe.
He installs windows. His new son's name

                        is something plain
as a pillar of salt. I am left now   to unscrew the bulbs
    from the ceiling of every room I'm in, their ruddy holiness
threatening dim wreckage
and shimmer. The scar where my stepfather widened
my smile,

                      still there.

The Thing About Fire

Growing Up, All the Mobile Homes

looked like orphan teeth in the Nevada
desert. As a boy I dragged myself street
by street, searched in every man's hand
for food, clothes, medicine.

I looked in every retired sky dragged
open and talking me into rough repair;
searched in the burning head wound
where my stepfather's steel hands

coaxed my mute blood out in puddles.
And those hands still haunt there
like a thorned crown threating to glow.
Every tree was tinder. What nothing is

left for treehouses. I hid in crawlspaces
with only earthworms for music
until I became old enough to know
what haunting was by listening

through the vents to all the thunder
about electrical bills, about who the fuck
is she, about silence after the dull
click as my mother's ribs caved,

that familiar sound of grief's keep,
its needed maintenance, singing along
to its own tradition; because I grew up
where graveyard homes baked deep

in the western heat, out the doors
like starved apertures came the choir
of mothers and sons, singing the human
death dance, the constancy of the poor.

This is the last time I'll write I grew up
where fathers levitated like electricity
in power lines, throaty hum constant,
tire fire kind of dangerous, the black eyes

my stepfather gifted me my mom momma
ma' please make a book of matches burn
for days like this, let the sky and earth reclaim
what they will of these wasted boxes, metal

bodies and waterless pine, reclaim our fathers
who holler in the street high on their want
for death, high above us like patron saints
of the hammer, of quick, clean brutality.

Prayer for This Kind of Hunger

I'm a little outside of myself this
Sunday. I haven't breathed right in
this summer's ouroboro. My son
crosses the street into its long
shadow, and I cook dinner anyway.
As a boy, I used to nix Sunday
sermons from the anointed men and
stuffed my mouth with them until I
overflowed with resurrection and
nails, as recklessly as my son rounds
the corner. But I was starving then,
and the churched faithful who
knotted themselves up at the edges
of my life told me hunger was the
reason for anything, even god. When
I slept, my slightened body against
my stepfather's chest, I could hear
my mother inside failing to open the
canned green beans with a rock.
Listen, we poor had something to say
about the names we kept
throatlatched. We kept invisible
ledgers of those who faded once and
for so long still, that consummation
of thievery and faith, the imprecise
how of hammering our lives into just
bones; how hard it's been to
remember the learned miracle of
tossing my blood into bloom over my
shoulder until a phantom rain wet

the sidewalk and choke cherry appeared. Listen, my son is interested in this kind of invocation and, like me, is a believer want for the semiundress of salvation. Listen, to my son curling back around the corner holding unknowing beautifully in his jaw; to the world behind him pressing forward, a tongue around a knifehandle. Inside, the names held in my teeth loosen bit by bit. They tie their boots and climb drowsy from my mouth and out the window. My son shuts the door and sits down at the table while I sharpen our only knife.

Brushfire #237 Outside of Reno, Nevada

> *When Bill McKibben declared "The End of Nature," in 1989,*
> *he was posing a hyperbolic kind of epistemological riddle: What*
> *do you call it, whatever it is, when forces of wilderness and weather,*
> *of animal kingdoms and plant life, have been so transformed by*
> *human activity they are no longer truly "natural"?*
> —David Wallace-Wells, *The Uninhabitable Earth.*

Right now, another fire in the haunted north
takes everything back — a piece of sky
the sky had no right to claim, the cattle-
field that is my father, old undergrowth
that is my mother, the coyote bone wind
chimes slung low on a ranch fence —
and this fire tells me it wants my son crowned
in thicket and soot. Later, this young king
will stand outside the pines, exhausted
from the already buckshot pocked west,
the razor-wired climate wrapped around
the rest of his life, this permanent
and inane serpent of rust and blood
and really what's the difference in this
metaphor anyhow? Both suggest someone,
once, was here, I guess? Weren't we
radiant? Anti-Anthropocene. Anti
gone until we become only self-filled
graves, our shovel hands heave once
toward the triple-six digits in the sky —
it's gonna be a scorcher, folks, in the re-origin
of species; please, the last one alive, turn
the lights off in this accidental furnace.

My son will feel birds tremble his mouth,
and a ladder flame hollowing him out
rung by rung at his middle, and I'll tell him
the bellied flames are just the last birds
of every fire on their way out. Don't be afraid
that I am afraid. Entire galaxies of light
will born from his mouth and for a moment
he will be radiant. He will be radiant.

Elegy for the West
– for J.

Windows stay dirty for months; belts of storms
shotgun against them, loud like little brothers.
The night pulls June bugs from out the mouths of hills.

The Russian olive is for windbreak, rain dark as pitch
where houses toddle on stilts to avoid the wash,
where violence sits across from every victim, feeds each

one wooden spools of wire to stitch up the graves inside.
Twelve years later, the same April shoots of primrose
sleep under starved cloud, forget and forget themselves

in the spaces between all the names for empty
that will never fill. These hills still sink and redden,
flush as clay in places under the granite fist of boulder

where the bracken of hands refuse to dig. In late winter
lamplight, winds from the haunted north hum
the darkness will nick your fingers into cheatgrass,

darling, and I knew it to be just true enough
to keep my knuckles tucked. I watched the hill
thieves as a boy, and the Black Crowned Night

Heron, too, lulled to sleep by a quarter moon,
thirsting. Outside the windows, a coyote chews a ghost-
ched bone in a desert that reaches into nothing.

Under this hard skin, life is buried too young, graves
filled with what moves through its children and too soon
to know the difference between our coins and eyes. Often,

we are ribboned into a knothole of memories that tie
us to the last unburned aspens – they rake in the sky,
like mother – with the great choiring of leaves.

My Son Asks Me, "Can I Use Science to See What Goes Through My Body?"

Somewhere the fields
still burn and I ask
the somewhere
if, nightly, like me,
it dreams of getting belly
down under the heat
before the flames
lick the damaged air
back out of my lungs.
The fields would say
nothing and open up
my face like a gate,
walk through without
closing it behind them.
My son stands just
outside the cut line,
hands palm up
and I become again
oblivion and breath,
move through him
quick as his mom
left and took flight
over this red field
where what is left
is a man made empty
by him being gone
and further from me
still. All I've wanted
is to wipe the blood,

dust from his feet,
before the scars take.
Tell him to come in
from the fields
and I'd wash our hands
in light that moves
through our bodies
as silent as uprisings
of ash.

Elegy for My Son in Rising Light

How often can I send my son to speak
to the emptiness inside the house
buried in woods before he comes back
with the wrong mouth, pulling honey
bees and dry oak out in knots, before
he begins to speak as the abandoned
house, speak as slow wind, speak
as half-collapsed roof kicked in
by a deliberate sky pouring itself
into him full and full still until stars
lit with what I now know to be dead
light glow inside his chest, speak
as a body drowned with sunrise.

My Son Asks Me, "Do You Remember When I Was Two?"

How could I forget
                   the only thing I haven't
wholly lost? Your crib

                                        I'd sleep below until you
           were old enough to not

                              need me to hold up that cage.
The taste of your mother's mouth
              the nickel of a revolver.

                         I've forgotten what it was
           like to towel your skin,
which is to say these hands
              are strangers to you now.
How I kept these hands
              over your head to save you
from thunder bringing

                    its body down. How I stuck
my fingers down your throat
           when you quit breathing
           and all I pulled out
           was a mistimed cry. What good
is it to tell you this? I have no
           right way to explain to you
                    why we become and become
                         again like lightning sparked
at the edge of a field, a small
bird bolted to a cage
              in its center, singing,
              then still.

Dear Nathan,

This morning I walked the top of a garage high in the middle of these casinos and watched another weekly motel go up in one long headstone-like plume; hurled itself toward a fleck of starlight and reminded me of how plain apocalypse looks when it comes to evict someone else's life into the sky; I mean, there's a lone bird needling through the smoke, stitching threads of deadgrey across it all to prevent more leaving. I'd been in this fever once, before I'd even tied string and a doorknob to my last tooth. We all grew up knowing that when the smoke comes, there would be less hungry mouths singing at school come Monday. Funny how song looks like a drowning gasp, the ecstatic when the ghost comes blundering out, like someone unseen reaching in to untie the children and send them aloft, you said. Today, I'm where the fathers of the gone fell asleep back to back to brace against the winds. Where yours wrapped you in a hundred hands and I reached out hoping he'd take me, too, away from the place where mine carved me from shed antler. Word is you now have your father's hands, that they're the red shade of earth when you untie me.

All I Want

My lungs to be brief, eventual.
To leak this body into a lake.
To come up twice for actual air.
Then. To disappear completely.
For this destruction to fill me.
To sink flat, be like god, enough.
My lips to ripen, swell into shores.
To be naked: slowtongued, emptier.
To be cleaned from the inside.
To be called back, for the living

I Ask Father Where We Are Driving

& in his clipped tongue he says,
your fever will break down outside
of Missouri, which is to say this length
between us will swell for states
and break down to avoid the chapped
runt-mouth of a forgotten tongue.
Somewhere outside

of this burnt out Buick, I want
to see it all: the way the homes
would wash away under storms
if it were not for the sidewalks
hardly holding them in their hills;
how a small box of animal teeth
has something to say about the way
we live; how brick & bone; how

I ask father what the street sign
says, how he repeats our new name;
how our name is not bird bone, not
hollow; not hallowed like flint
in winter, but holy like lies
from father in fever sweats, like
what's ripped in the backseat looks
like my mother's only dress; how
he spoke was how I buried him, low

swamp shallow; how my fever was a kind
of life briefly; how he pulled off license plates
before we crossed the Missouri border; how
the dead enter our mouths; how we hold
their names like nails in our teeth. Whatever
keeps the jaw clenched shut enough.

A Soft Fugue

Father breathes himself into a yard,
breathes himself larger at the edge of my
tongue, breathes himself into a bang in
the muzzle of a six-gun. Such is the world.
Flash. Recoil. Quiet. He then sleeps and
sleeps on the lawn, his body an exit wound
in the world. I breath, I silence, open up
the wound with sticks, find a soft fugue
and other still life, push it all through
until there's nothing but a hollow and an
astrolabe in blaze. My father once told me
that the thoughts of youth are slender, no
a misshapen hazard, no, they're the
disguise of prayer where we mean to make
love, son, no, where we mean to make
ourselves empty. No, the thoughts of youth
are where we follow each other until we
glisten with failure, no, they're as sharp
as the double-helixed concertina wire he
buried deep in my mother, no, it's the rope
that pulled her tiny life into that muted
dark. This mouthless thing, this unnoise
where I daily bottle my father's ashes and
hang them from a tree for Magpies to
trouble against; where I sit at the always-
emptying edge of his bedside, press my
head against the shape of my mother as she
stands above me, disrobed of life. I breast
her with my hands. I kiss and kiss soft the
new spaces in two red blooms.

My Son Asks Me, "Do All Rivers Go to the Edge of the World?"

Two months after he asks this, I walk
the river alone behind my house and imagine
I answer that I taught myself to swim
in a river just like this when I was a boy:
hollyhock rust at the edge, my father
set back in pines, his eyes hollowing,

waving the way that looks like drowning.
I imagine if my son were with me
we'd walk over a bridge like a ribcage,
and he'd cover his ears to mute the sound
of rain swelling the river upward, mute

the sounds of tongues in thirsting shoreline
pines demanding we dance. And dance
to what? The sound of a world round
with us over this water that struggles
to disappear and he'd look at me

with glow that says this should be home,
that says he could live here by the river
with me and I'd agree, and he'd grab sticks
to try to make the home I couldn't.
I'd tell him I'm sorry that I never got

the windows right, that his mother
had a voice that blew in glass; reckless
storm, love, gunshots, and so on.
I would try to tell him I'm sorry I was
dopesick when he was an earthquake

and his mom was round with him inside her
and he moved her landscape, mountains
of his fists pushing her stomach skyward,
threatening to split. I would try to tell him
that I once stuck the hungry aperture

of a handgun down a man's mouth
for a tiny bit of infinity balled up black
in balloons and pulled a voice from out
that thinned throat. But all I could do is point
two fingers at that storm overhead and hope

for a lightning's slow rumble to move through
us. He likes stories about handmade handguns
and birthday balloons and he'd remember
when he was sick once too and I stayed up
for three nights beating his fever back

with these dangerous hands and he'd think
these stories are happy because he trusts
the nature of my hands is to heal
and he'd ask why I let the water out
of my face when I tell him about the man

I was days before I first held him the way
streets wear magpies with their roadkill,
in need, and I'd say it's because how else
can I apologize, save for the same way
the rain's heavy fists coax the ground

downstream, like fathers, like sons, slipped
down, cleaved into these parts like him
and me and he vanishes and that sound
choirs through these bones where I walk
this gulf alone with the deadening storm.

Ode to My Son Circling Fallen Dark

I sent my son into a muted corral
outline in the chalkdry desert
and he came back with hands full
bloom with the rakish wingtips
of a frigatebird and a stomach full
of Russian thistle; he came apart
at the shoulder socket and flew
like only the left wing of a bird;
he detached at the root, rolled
like heat breathed up toward
a rioting dark break of dusk,
forgetting when I pressed him
against my chest like a second
heart, how he cleaved me open
to tumble in, hide from the long
night I sent crawling after him.

Self-Portrait with Palms

I have suffered
        near enough this March—
for to break, then break
        more, for to swallow
my disease,
        for to fuck my hand
again dry and tired,
        spit blood and pieces
of bone into my palm
        before I shake hands
with men who all have
        my father's face, to enter
deep into that riot
        in our palms, pull
my knotted name
        out, pull my mother
from the field where
        she is bent under
the rubble of broken thunder—
        is to call this
my life and burn it
        down black around me,
is to tuck ashes
        in the pocket between
gum and lip, taste
        the fire, misfortune.
Around the corner,
        March peels itself
away from the sky
        in shavings. I try

to find my face where
  I slick back my teeth
and kneel in front
  of my father, where
rain licks the street
  black, that proper
shade of burial.

Aubade for Ma' with De La Soul
—For 1989

My ma' loves daisies, their push upward. She wakes
with bees strictly to be stuck with honey on her tongue;
swollen, the bees sing her soul thick and she chokes
on the flecked light that mirrors break into. Our nights
break in two; the back of a mouth that wails nightly;
her darker eyes war with the blackbirds on the corner.
It's the fourth of July. The skies in confetti

         crashes. It's 1989
and I'm five, no, I'm more in bloom than that; I'm father
-less the first time the radio bangs me out my sleep. I wait
for ma' to climb down from the rooftop, scarved
in pipe smoke 'til the break of dawn drowns this orphan
city in light. Who has not been high exalted by mothers
above them who purse pistols meant for a sky, where fire
-works boom, flower into coronas, and born young rulers?

I Found Hiding is a Darker Thing That Keeps Us

I found myself in a friend's jeans, then his hand.

I found my father asleep. I broke him into bread.

I found mother with a cock in her mouth. Laugh.

I found for the first time the ornament of tongue.

I found myself in attic fire. Loss is too full of itself.

I found how my father's knuckles tasted in prayer.

I found him mouthless, ornamented in thick black.

I found this is the place where I throat my silence.

I found my son in a thicket. Half-thorned/throned.

I found bolt-cutters. I feel better now about mercy.

I found prostration. Still, now, I've not apologized.

I found all I've needed in the air's nicked wounds.

I found all I've needed in a truck stop bathroom.

I found my want for crucifixion is how I make love.

Bullet Hole in My Stepfather's Neck and Finally
I Write Love into a Poem

Son, I said I'd tell you the truth, this is part of it: I married your mother so you would be born more whole than I was. My father was gone before the sun dried the blood on my mother's thighs into a Rorschach bloom. This is the only west I've ever known. Where prophets – each one a glaciation of grief carving sluice grafts through the city – have all since died or stand sentry on the corner of 4th and Ralston under a sutureless sky waiting for anything – ascension, a cigarette, an open hand because palm readers don't work fists. My grandfather framed my face with his thumb-thick glasses as boy and pointed me like some directional device toward the horizon's orison, that ritual burial of light. He said, *probably it's a drop of blood blossoming.* Probably I now chase the bottom of every bottle and know only to call a sunset *a good harm.*

By now your mom has probably told you I laid hands on her. I did, but only in supplication. I saw my grandfather do this once to a boy who was snakebit up the street. After, he pressed his mouth against the boy's arm to draw the poison nearer to the surface. This is how I learned to kiss. Listen. Don't let anyone tell you that you can't say love. This is the only time I've ever said it full and meant it. My stepfather taught me love meant the scar from a bullet blowing the confetti out the side of his neck, meant the warmth when he finally let me run my finger over it the night before my sixth birthday. I was the same age as you are now. I want you to know love means both incredibility and immutable fear, means the hole in the world after the sky returns the bullet, means so much wait, and how I've waited so long for you and you're gone across the country and I still watch the sky for the bulletbreak and tumble. In the picture you keep of me nailed above your bed, I had cotton fever and was shaking through. In it, my eyes are not mine but belonged then to an impossible dark I was looking back toward. If your mom says that you have my eyes, know that she's wrong. Throw rocks through them when you read this, love. Give no warning.

When I Dreamt Only in the Colors of Cempasúchitl
—after Roger Reeves

Each night on the phone, my son slips into wind.
Each morning, he raises a forest to his lips,

drinks the hennaed light through the pines.
Look, his hands are two warring miracles,

his body a fulcrum to raise the earth around him
until he breaks. But there is no sound in this moment.

Over time his body becomes river-shore where trees
that make the best light-canoes to quit the land in

keep splitting and the grain can't keep straight,
and the tumblehome is wrong and the river wars

with dead horses it's called back home. I carry this
coalition of bereavement on a gunshot breeze,

cross the boundary waters, the animal that I am,
stack my bones neatly like this, spilled salt at dusk.

Tonight, But with Wolves

We call this a wanting place. The men's feet
have split against the dusk-cold. Their simple
blood borns a mosaic in the sand and the ground
says it's lucky to have it and it is. Their knees are clean
shot through and they dance until wind
strings the holes with a sick melody – the kind
of song that patrols, say, the air around wild
horse hunts, or a harvest of bees in their last sigh
toward collapse – which becomes our next
year's weather and then a fortune tellers' spell
at an hourly rate, of course, and polyester
flowers and a rope of kerchiefs for next year's
forgetfulness. But the crops don't abide
and my family hungers again and we sentinel
our ritual burn barrel, pregnant now with flame.
The boy opposite me looks like the low fire
tore at his fur looks like the fire and inconsolable
looks like me except the eyes are wrong
and his edges blur. The superstitious among us
call him an apparition, a jinx. The others, uninitiated
in the desert might call him a mirage, a swollen,
ambulatory thirst. But you know this
is wrong. If I get close enough, I might reach into
where his eyes should be, grab ahold of the river
in them, the one water left in the west, I've heard,
and drop it between us. Flames turn each of our faces
into stop lights on red where the boy and I collide.
The honeyed smoke – our white trash offering
to the gods of all that – bands in choked braids,
something umbilical and therefore hungrier

than whatever circles the perimeter fence.
The wolves came back dressed in a bewilderment
of teeth. They do like this in the cold season
to solve, I think, a hidden compromise
that holds the space between the barrel
and our incorrectly gravitied bodies. And so,
we toss gifts into the barrel to forgive us
their surge; a storebought Christmas
tree – the plastic kind – with fishhooks affixed
to a child's emptyheaded craft ornaments
and burning star for tree-topper; my younger
brother's pill bottle rattle; what remains
of the chickens after the winds came
after the heat came after the derelict night came
and then stayed. The high desert has no patience
for dead languages, seasonal ghosts or myth,
which is a childhood disease. But so too,
I guess, is drought, which believes so purely
in us that it's settled in lengthwise
with entire mountains in its teeth and bulges
simply to admire its own permanence. The newsman
says it's the driest January since the beginning
of records, but who can be concerned
when there's song here? And the men insist
on this last song, and percussion the dim circle
with handgun rounds. They lick the sky
in this final act of longing. How close to god
and still hungry. But the night stretches on
indifferently, a sallow rider galloping toward
poisoned water we let loose while we were too busy
falling in love until it vanished.

We Were Not There

Portrait of a Breakup Through Scenes Taken From Las Vegas

How many centuries must have elapsed before men reached the point of
seeing any other fire than that in the sky?
         — Jean-Jacques Rousseau

A man matchstrikes a wig at the doors of Saint Paul the Apostle's Church, singing we outgrew the old god; this suicide king climate, played out and bayonetted on the horizon, a shrike tight-roping barbedwire with a new kill; soft pupils nickeled under casino lights, all cartoon stars and slack fugue in the last six months of August; if you look closer through the local children's eyes, they imagine synchronized swimming in lakes of mercury with distorted reflections of themselves but these kids they begin drowning because nobody learns to swim in a drought and the people on shore think they're waving while they sink and they wave back while hollering, make your own luck; alfalfa and alkali flats and bodies and bodies flailskirt Hoover Dam; the Mojave fat with stillborn wind; neo-pointillism in the carpets of Caesar's Palace the only agitprop that could ever matter; U.S. 95 leaves in no direction at all with a bindlestiff of undocumented bones carved into loaded dice; the dusk giving up again on the Armargosa; cutthroats on The Strip with Three-card Monte draw chalk outlines on the bottoms of each and step through leaving their shadows behind; town criers with jackets full of off-brand doves; Boulder Highway opens up like the Sawing a Woman in Half gag without the laugh-track or awe and we stand on both sides; used car salesmen sprout and swivel in the traffic wind; the casinos and hotels mar and glisten, lick the lines of the horizon, and likely, too soon, will turn headstone and therefore permanent; Yucca Flat; downwinders; down and outers; honeymooners kiss their phantom limbs and the breeze beading over their torn ghosts; knots of faithful in smoking Buicks outside 24-hour wedding chapels, Elvises in Presbyterian white suits half razzle bedazzled with cigarette burns, holding solander bible and guitar; late-stage Dionysus with a pack of non-filters waist deep in the second shift at the video store; night owls with eyeholes like onyx at all night diners fill their gullet coffers with steak and egg specials and puzzle over a child's carving of a smiley face in the booth bench; a woman just over there, almost out of sight, pushes her station wagon through an intersection flashing red flashing red flashing red flashing

After Viewing John Maguire's Painting *Montgomery Street in Winter*

Painting: birch, brick, chimney
stuck through apartment, fence,
shed stamped with snow, creek,
tendons of ice and ash, Studebaker
out of frame (not running), sky.

We say nothing driving from a garage sale
somewhere between Reno and Donner,
the water-gashed interstate, zippered
on either side by pine, telephone poles,
and gray, carnelian in places where rain
meets oil and needles of autumn, drink in
the silence, abandon this map, navigate
by a catalog of blues and cold, drive further
into stale air and December, harder into 1996.

But no, you were not there. We were not there.
No stump of tree, no grass or sky, but bills,
apartment, lamp, porcelain. You said nothing.
I said non-photo blue when I should have said
knuckle of bone, winter.

After Hearing Zachary Schomburg's *The Book of Joshua*
—For Mathias Svalina

So much of what I've written
has been a lie. What I know:

a poet scratched a picture of me
into the title page of his book

the other night after a reading
where ghosts rose from a radio,

no, two radios, and the drawing
was a shirt buttoned to the top

without a head or anything else
and this was sincere. I could see

it in how his hands shook against
the book named after him. I can't

tell him just how much I appreciate
being disappeared in a picture

of myself. But I can't say anything
without a face. He said he dared not

name me and I stuffed a cigarette
into his mouth to celebrate him

making anything of me. The other
night, after the reading, with a pen

I drew in the rest of my vanished
body: a pile of sticks wrapped neat

with a ribbon of sympathy; an ex-
plosion skirted up from the ditch

of the neckhole; break a leg, he said,
and so I drew in hammers for legs,

break into beleaguered light, he said,
and red flashbangs fired from out

of where my head was supposed
to be thinking that its disappearance

is odd-shaped; what does a man
with no arms do except for sink

a little quicker? I wanted to say
please come a little closer, please

hold me up and make me a little
more honest by letting me go

home. Stay here, form the night,
which is absence, buttoned up.

Of Stone and Glass

Tomorrow the wind
will fold me sideways
into my desk. Tomorrow
I will break into a fever
of counting: forty-two
homes outside my window,
two dozen hotel pen caps,
a paper, envelope, my name
twice written on it—
one in cursive, the other
a series of mirrors
above it—, a picture
of a girl and I blooming
the corners of our mouths.

Tomorrow I will begin
to guess a violent kind
of guessing, like naming
what's empty, while I
imagine that she is now
older, that she's now
somewhere up sidewalk
or street or ribboned inside
herself a little further back
in the dogmouth hills, her
dry heave of breath, thirsting.

As kids we would kiss
in those hills our fathers
worked. They aged, forgot
to bury themselves. We
kissed, forgot ourselves
into ourselves, forgot
the sound of our lips, stone
against glass, a break of tooth
against tooth. Us, wrapped
hard in each other's fists.

I think of her chest, mine,
halved, opened on hinges,
heaved wide into the air
of a history we mistook.
I think lost. I think of mouth
and mouth and that if I listen
close enough I might hear
them bang together, break
like bone cages, break
like stone, like window.

Still Life with a Hollow in It
—For Bob Hicok

My favorite poet asked me
what I am ardentheartedly
afraid of: that I am lacking,
that even now I ask him
for permission and I am
afraid of what follows me home
at night; I find myself bent
whenever my shadow grows
too long. I fear I've become
easier to ignore, that I am
merely someone else's word
for vanish. The first time

I saw myself entirely
was in a nixed polaroid
my stepfather kept in his
pocket of my mother giving
birth to me. Crowned, that's
what it's called, right? King
me. This is not a metaphor.
My head never lost the blood
and noise in its dents. My mother
is still alive, I think. I am still
in the picture, and even though
I hung up the phone years ago,
my mother is still screaming

for me to come home.
I thought then if I pushed

enough with a small finger
I could unmake myself.
I scissored a hole just wide
enough for me to fit through,
then disappear completely.
There is no translation for where
I ought to appear in the photo
breached, backbodied, kinged,
mother wrapped around me.

For My Stepfather, With Teeth Painted

When he'd sleep off his scrapped knuckles
and the pieces of my head caught in his skin,
I recalled people from his bar stories,
fashion ink from ash and my urine,
and paint his teeth: the tiny blind woman
on the corner with an umbrella and dull coins
for eyes; the man with two obsidian
9mms tattooed on his waist, who, later,
will help my stepfather cut three fingers
off some nameless man for something less
than free; Hitchcock, and pigeons in the bar
parking lot my stepfather aimed his gunhand
at when drunk. BANG. I painted a handmade
handgun and a soft ring of feathers. BAAANG.
His canines are all men with hammers and bone
saws. Each hammer tempered from bad origins
and graveyards for firstborns.

My son is beginning to paint pastorals; of fathers
and sons strung like rabbit carcasses to the pines,
which lean closer to each other in the wind
to tell secrets meant to be overheard; he paints
when we feed the dog together, paints three-dozen
elk growing into hollyhocks at the world-cliff,
paints toys that, like me, have bad origins,
that, like magic tricks, are cut in half for applause.

Back Home

My beloved tells me our red hook summer's over. The world
outside scabs itself over with a new winter flesh.
Our first summer together, a boy from the dive
tried to gift me a bullet, but it refused me and so I stayed
in a slick dream with her a little longer. I opened her door,
the morning reached over the desert, and she held me
in my blood. We swayed on the porch to the gospel
of the morning traffic, those first responders
to light. Our shadows resurrected somewhere else entirely.
The blood dried and years later, we learned to spend time
between wars gathering in rapture, in bursts of blown-out
light annexing our home. We styled these wars
with shrapnel gowns just past the color of release.
I used to fatten myself with survivor's guilt, that salted face
on a black horse I kneeled before to worship until the rider,
pallid and not unlike me, dismounted and reached into
my solar plexus to pluck a dandelion, make a bomb of it,
and evacuate everyone from around me. No, this is a lover's
guilt; a carefully sifted night where there's no exit
except through a field of blackberries where we left my son
to gather fruit and leave impossible gems of blood
on the thorns. I pressed my thumb, split and heaving
from the briar hooks against her lips in some dumb attempt
to stop time. What's unsaid is on god. Absolve me, despite
everything. What other explanation can there be?
This is how I imagine life in a last wash across my tongue.
And, even now, I look above the briar, to the season's
rising vapor, where it takes to the air in fleeces, sheets
over the sky like some curious god wishing to rise
and stare down at us, ghostface to ghostface. We retreated

into a quiet storm, into a hundred years lined on both sides
with darkened candle wicks, into a flag of ordinary violence
wilted on its pole trying to flee the haunted skyline. I too lived
where we intended to raise the dead. Do you remember
when we danced to "Unchained Melody" and the walls leaned
forward to thank us for lighting a pallet-fire in the center
of the room and we twirled one stubborn cold season
into another until even the wars stopped for fear of becoming
their own ghosts and the shadows multiplied and imitated
our tender, wrongheaded steps and eventually they walked out
of the dim walls and watched? We too lived, where a hymnal
of shadows, not unlike us, pressed forward, singing bell-
flowered, afraid of nothing, undressed like a bullet.

How I Make Sense of Miscarriage

In each room I'm in I draw a door in chalk
on the floor, draw stairs, sketch a crude
closed slidebolt, shut it all behind me. Stay here,
sweetheart. Before I leave on a hard blade
of morning, she rattles the window, I snuff out
morning's cigarette in a flowerpot, she pulls
tiny shoulders and ribs from between her legs,
reads the Lives of Animals, she writes: Dear
Darkness, forgive our young, and us, their thieves.

Where We Place Our Hands

A low, thundering ache claps slow
applause in my partner's stomach.
I listen to the clamor grow larger
and imagine it's a plane taking off
too low over this dozing Seattle suburb
where its engines will cough
something black out its back, begin
its tumble into later when it gives
up everything, becomes something
like the ground but more furious.

I think how maybe the whole way down
a woman kept a chirruping little thing,
some warm bones perhaps, against
her breast, how she didn't make a single
noise as the boy in seat next to her
was pulled out by a sky not knowing
it was hungry until the plane started
to leave it, and that woman, looking
out the window, maybe imagines
her husband cleaning pool filters
of carrion below her, maybe

looking like my mother after the crib
killed her second son, blankets
wrapped sweetly and completely
around him, and the woman pushed
that boy deep and deep until it became
a gem in her chest and it glowed
with grief and swelled until that grief

became like a boy with a mouth wishing
for its wail.

This is all I know after my partner and I
decided to not have children. That boy.
Any boy unmade by disaster.
And I'm unmade now as I hover my hand
over the soft dells of her belly and the shadow
on the adjacent wall takes the shape of a plane
but the ceiling keeps the plane from taking
too high and it loops above her
and becomes a ball in the air, glows

with its own heart and swells
only the way fists can, and I push it inside
her stomach and let that dumb heart
blossom, let it mistake, let the whine
from the engines and mothers wake
my son asleep in fits in the next
room with planes in his head.

In Thinking About Divorce, I Climb Trees

It's been almost two decades since I've
climbed any trees. I scratched *trouble will
find you* into one and lost my footing
somewhere around the top near sundown.
On my way toward forgetting my face at
the bottom, each branch that kissed my
bones in halves became a year until I'd
collected enough years to fill my hands
with the rest of my life. I'm not old, though
the tongue-pink in my hands would
argue otherwise. I climbed with a girl once.
We played pretend married. I, with a job at
the garage building Iron Giants. I'd lost a
finger, of course. And she was careful not
to hold that hand too tight. Her,
preternaturally smarter than me, smoked
cigarettes behind the 7-11 like our mothers.
We were both 10. And I pushed her out
into the sky. If beauty and grace are the
bend and the snap, then I think what I
wanted was the girl turned into air, at least
something more ascendant than the dirt lot
at the abandoned volunteer fire station she
pinwheeled toward. But all she did was fall
and fall until she burned with the leaves on
the ground and then she just kept on
falling. And all I learned then, and now, is
that I can't apologize. I still see her from
time to time, as she careens past my
kitchen window when I'm finishing dishes.
I wasn't married then, as I am now, though

not for much longer because we don't agree
on the merits of recycling or the theory of
gravity or its practical applications or not
fucking each other differently than prostrate
or climbing trees to escape Sisyphusian days
on loop on loop or, finally, an unbraided
future, with me in clamber-up trunks to try
again to become godsized, as boys mostly
cannot do, again miss a limb, make some
grandeur out of falling.

More of the Day Collapses

A woman walks by, deep in autumn
and on fire, naked against both the sky
and asphalt. She drags her mother's
hips behind her, head antlered with gold
and too full of noise. She wears a coat
made of something from misery—
wool perhaps—and a band of fabric,
sideways from neck to wind, a sun
scarved with cloud. Her one hand
is a key; blade, bow, bittings. The other
is a letter; enveloped, postdated, written
in pencil, stamped with skin. I think of her

there, at her mailbox looking up here,
not at her mailbox, where I watch
bird-like, clumsy, think of how we might
unzip our skulls, again pull the stitches
of our lips back against each other,
abandon this distance and run every red
light on our way out of town, take up
dousing in the blithe desert and vanish.
But that's not the story. The story is that
this is not a poem as much as it is a thief,
lines lifted from our memory, anchored
to an anvil of bone, knotted to a string
tied to you now reading this somewhere
forward from me now, tied to a postdated letter
she slipped in her back pocket, never mailed.
It's still October.

In Which I Passively Participate in Two Suicides

A blizzard harasses the drought and a pack
of mules in the desert. Outside, the night is revived

into a different flesh, quieter, I'm in the last
apartment I'll ever live in with my wife. I'm outside

the bathroom door where I listen to her conjure
ghosts and storm clouds opposite and the rubble

of her small body collapses onto a blade. My son
watches cartoons downstairs. I will know later

what my younger sister must've felt to discover
our brother hanging like a ceiling fan

turned on low in the garage. Did she think
about why his fingernails were painted the color

of just past midnight or if she will forget her
own name, or his, as sometimes I do? I don't mean

to be insensitive. Forgive me. Sister, forgive
the ceiling. I would've forgotten my name,

too, as I have forgotten how to hold my sister
sincerely. Not because I don't love her,

but because I have this dream so often
that she stands below him and the rope is gone,

and they both tell me how beautiful I am
for stopping by unannounced. My wife prepares

the knife I'll have to forgive for making her bodiless
on the other side of this door where all I hear

is the noise she keeps her hair neatly wrapped in.
She will unravel herself like everyone else

from around my life, the way a ballet slipper
twists into some bloody, unremarkable pink.

Downstairs, a snake filches food from Felix
the Cat and a cartoon downpour drowns it all out

and a crane appears stage left with a beak-full
of kittens and her cries upstairs become a scatter

of birds at first light. Given the word, I'd drop
vine seeds into her wrists, let roots take hold

to sew the brawled space shut. I would use the knife
to open a hole in the ceiling to plead uselessly

with the storm. Outside, the snow has taken
everything hostage. My son stops his cartoons.

He walks outside, asks what the storm wants.
It turns to him. My son holds his hand out.

In Which a Child's Game Empties Me

This is our game: my son reaches
into a sackcloth, I close my eyes,
he pulls out two fists: one an evening
of war in the square of his jaw (I taught
him this), the other a bellbreak for children
of ruin. There are only so many metaphors
for loss. He holds both hands behind
his back. His face is the ritual first quiet
of an avalanche while he waits for me.
Guess what hand you're in, daddy?
He always lets them open, a windswept
distance when he releases his fists
and nothing but silence and wait falls out.

Forecasting

When I write, "I am weathering out"
I mean this is how I further disassemble:
my chin scar reopens the way ruddered
boats blade and peel back lakes, (out
with my bones) and back (out now
with my clouded voice) and back (out
with the abandoned continent of my face),
then, too, the constellations of my body
become both the sky and reflection
in a shallow lake pooled in the Sawtooth
above this burnt version of earth. I mean
a red booted cooing boy with rocks
in his fists will see all of this happen
and rain me out in darkening celebration,
make some use of me finally. When I write,
"we need to dig deeper wells, the earth
keeps falling in" I mean those stones
will ruin me so far out and further still
until I douse the everyday brushfire
that's burning in that boy's backyard
since I left and made desolation
out of already desert. I mean I just want
to become everywhere to be nearer
to him, even if it takes me apart fully.

My Son's Self-Portrait with Black Crayon

My son is six and losing teeth. After
brushing the soft pits in his mouth he cries
and I try to sing him to sleep as he's afraid
of coming apart from his mouth out
and the gravel in my throat makes the song
sound of a nightjar being buried inside of me.

—

Yesterday I turned fevered and hummed
to him while he pressed his hands
where my eyes are. He hides my face like this
every time before I leave. Today I left him
in the haunted west. How else can I explain
what it's like to lose a child to distance?
Fatherhood? To walk under an impossible sky?
Every sky is a weight and I can't save you
from it throwing itself down onto your body?
Thieves? A hush of light before a duststorm?

—

He told me the other day that the future
is blank and white. I asked him
where he heard this from. He opened
his mouth, pulled crayons out in a bag, drew
a picture of the future which was square,
filled it in black and black and black, said,
you aren't here.

My Son Asks Me, "How Does the Earth Grow the Graves?"

Absolutely. Blushing. Bits
        of earth, gladiolas,
                finding their way up
With god too busy cleaning
        his new kill
                to be bothered to turn
around when called in
        for dinner. At 9:15
                in the morning
funeral, tomorrow's,
        too. With Patsy
                Cline or your mother
walking after someone
        after midnight after
                she unties herself from a diner
and where love leaves
        in a stranger's semi,
                pretty lights trailing.
With mispronounced
        silence becoming
                salience, sirens, séance;
with hope a face
        will come back full
                buoying to the surface
after too much time
        feeding the appetite
                of a lake. With brass

knuckles making meals
       out of teeth; soft belly
              aches after kissing
that hard. With a thresher
       waiting long for mistake
              to fall in front of it.
With lightning falling
       in love for a moment
              with our skin before
forgetting its fear
       of being vulnerable
              and abandoning us
for the sky.
       With the husk
              of a deer skull
being made
       into a skinned home
              for magnolias. Later
it will be used
       as a still-life model of less
              in the way the hunt
is less
       a field-dressed animal,
              more the blade's edge
taking its time loving
       that body. With bodies,
              our bodies, in need
to feel love take up
       inside us the way
              hunger takes up residence

in a wintered family
        when the snow stops
                the fields and hope
begins knitting a fire
        place in their stomachs
                and those new spaces
are still never warmed.
        With this scene:
                the only time
I was late to pick
        my son up from school
                and on our way home
walking under a hateful
        rain that threatened
                to pull our skin down
we stopped
        at a hollowed-out stump
                where someone planted
peonies and marigolds
        and all I could do,
                all I can do,
is point
        to that moment.

Boyhood with Low Hum from the Burn Field

Still as pinned-down moth wings, the daylight
      drowns down slower. My family's broken

down fleet of junkyard cars are in their move
      toward rust, that color of oblivion. Further out

still, a midday-insomniac sagebrush field where
      skin learns how it's skin, the gentle flush,

two boys hold a rabbit skull and each other's
      sunlicked ribs, miniatures of their fathers

in cupped hands; both resemble trembling.
      Where are the boys I remember who tightened

air harder between them? Who played a rigged
      dice game with death, that Goya shadow

at the low edge of the burning field of youth?
      We learned to toss bones from a cup, interpret

the space widening between like some knotted
      maze not meant to be solved. Where are the boys

who tightroped each other just above a tank
      of black pitch? Their one hidden skin porcelain

thick pouring over each other. I need the sky
      here, darkening about their brows. I need that

somewhere to release its ropes, curtaining
        glimmer off their backs. Before the summer

quits, they follow a deer path through the field,
        arms outstretched to grow wings, they bank

side to side, against the glow and flight
        of their bodies, away, and always back. Boys

in arc. Boys become gravity and pulse,
        until they're home and sentried by silence,

the whitetrash car garden bed down, moonlit.
        I carried the skull to sleep. And that's all it was:

I learned love amongst bones and wreckage.
        I arranged my bones around love and wreckage.

I became wreckage, wreckage, on and on.

Acknowledgments

Sincere gratitude to the editors of the journals and anthologies in which these poems have appeared:

The Meadow: "After Viewing John Maguire's Painting *Montgomery Street in Winter,*" "More of the Day Collapses"

Muzzle: "Self-Portrait with Palms," "Elegy for the West," "Self-Portrait with a Hollow in It"

Tahoma Literary Review: "Growing Up, All the Mobile Homes"

Taos Journal of International Poetry and Art: "My Son's Self-Portrait with Black Crayon," "Elegy for a Son in Rising Light," "My Son Asks Me, 'Do You Remember When I Was Two?'", "My Son Asks Me, 'Can I Use Science to See What Goes Through My Body?'", "All I Wanted," "Prayer for this Kind of Drought"

Thrush: "Of Stone and Glass"

Vinyl: "A Soft Fugue"

Waxwing: "I Ask Father Where We Are Driving," "I Found Hiding is a Darker Thing That Keeps Us"

"A Soft Fugue" was selected by Jamaal May for the 2014 Emily Morrison Prize in Poetry

"Growing Up, All the Mobile Homes" was nominated for Best New Poets 2015

"How I Make Sense of Miscarriage" was selected for the 2015 Creativity and Medicine Prize

"Aubade for Ma' with De La Soul" appear in the anthology It *Was Written: Poetry Inspired by Hip-Hop* (Minor Arcana Press, 2016)

Notes + Paraphernalia

Notes + Paraphernalia

My Mother and Father Were Astronauts plays footsy with nonfiction. It takes its title from Seven Star's 2004 album of the same name. This is a cartography of some of my folk, a psychogeographical junction in a roadmap drawn with crayon. This poem references Francisco Goya's Black Painting, *Saturn Devouring His Son*. The phrase "say the black" is extracted from the phrase "say the black, do the red" in catholic orthodoxy. It marks a tension in our obligation to interior monologue and exterior makings-of-things. To "say the black" on loop is to yank on that thin thread of fidelity to interior truths. This poem is the book's black-as-pitch orientation.

Growing Up, All the Mobile Homes is a nonfiction poem. The line "food, clothes, medicine" references Aesop Rock's song of the same name on his 2005 album, *Fast Cars, Danger, Fire and Knives*.

Prayer for This Kind of Hunger is for my son on the anniversary of us living alone together for the first time. Sometimes he turns the corner out of sight and comes back to me older and less of me and I'm wrought up and in glow simultaneously.

Brushfire #237 Outside of Reno, Nevada was written in the summer of 2020 when west coast fires bloated into indifferent eaters and the smoke came and settled in everything. Who could've envisioned the apocalypse dressed in an understated tangerine glow. David Wallace-Wells has written extensively about displaced climate anxiety taking the shape of handsome men in dystopian fiction as a result of both denialism and scientific reticence; the banal spectacle of it all blossoming from the bankruptcy of imagination.

My Son Asks Me, "Do You Remember When I Was Two?" is for my son and younger brother. After my brother was born, I took to sleeping under his crib as a means of protecting him from ghosts. I resumed this ritual after my son was born. I bought a Santissima Muerte candle for the first time during his second year.

Dear Nathan is dedicated to Nathan and Aschley, both of whom have kept me in the world.

All I Want echoes Tomas Tranströmer.

I Ask Father Where We Are Driving reimagines my stepfather's actual exile to South Dakota. The reality is that I was left bloodied in a driveway in 1996. I haven't heard from him since. I did, once, on a 2015 road trip from Virginia to Nevada, find his home address down the street from the hotel I was in. I parked in front for a spell and played "Gimme Shelter" on loop.

A Soft Fugue is for Christmas Eve, 1994.

Aubade for Ma' with De La Soul is for her hundred hundred hearts.

I Found Hiding is a Darker Thing That Keeps Us is the delirious heart-shaped parallax object of this book.

Bullet Hole in My Stepfather's Neck and Finally I Write Love into a Poem is a nonfiction poem.

Tonight, But with Wolves began with a burn barrel. These eaters are a simple and critical central artifact of life in the country.

Portrait of a Breakup Through Scenes Taken From Las Vegas: El-P. "TOJ." *Fantastic Damage*, Definitive Jux, 2002.

After Hearing Zachary Schomburg's The Book of Joshua is for Seattle, 2014.

Of Stone and Glass is for Reno.

Still Life with a Hollow in It is a nonfiction poem. This photo was kept in a bedside drawer in my parents' room, alongside shotgun shells and occasional bags of ditch-weed.

For My Stepfather, With Teeth Painted vacillates between nonfiction and magic realism. Choose your own adventure, I guess. The first man I ever fear (read: worshipped at a safe distance) rode an ancient Harley and had two black-as-pitch pistols tattooed on his waistline, as to give the appearance that they were half-concealed. I never understood whom he was hiding this one art from. This man and my stepfather orchestrated bareknuckle boxing matches between me and the other boys in the empty lot abutting their burnt-out Victorian for some handfuls of dollars. The kids placed side bets in the brush before the fights, using sticks to write out these contracts in the dirt before each spitting onto the earth to turn the contract to covenant. Whoever won had to bring the other boys gifts to school on Monday. I always brought wildflowers if the season was right.

Back Home is To: Suzy, From: Sam.

How I Make Sense of Miscarriage is as close as I can get. Apology never satisfies the holes that constellate our lives.

Where We Place Our Hands was written following a partner's miscarriage.

More of the Day Collapses is for Reno, 2008.

In Which I Passive Participate in Two Suicides is for my brother, Devin, and my sister, Alishia; I'd wolf anything to preserve you both. This poem was written on the anniversary of my brother's re-entry into the before and after.

My Son's Self-Portrait with Black Crayon is, obliquely, a non-fiction poem.

Boyhood with Low Hum from the Burn Field is proximal hope. Amidst all the calamity and skittery fear that pock the lives of boys raised by men who were raised by hammers, there were and are moments where the transient embodiment of love takes up in curious forms. This poem is the book's **accidental animus, and a magician's gesture toward wonder, toward awe, a thumb tracing the scars grafting this boy's body.**